Fahm al-Qawā`id

Start learning how to spell & read the *Qur`ān*!
Starting from *Alif Bā Tā*, then words & their meanings!

Foundation Entry Level - Arabic Alphabets & Words

A new Qaidah for a new way of learning *alhamdulillah Fahm al-Qawā`id* 2019 ©
Learning the letters of Arabic, vowel signs & translations of words.
Perfect choice for learning & teaching from the very beginning.

Learn & Understand
Qaida with Meanings

المستوى الأول / Level (1)

Providing Quality Educational Resources. A Book for Adults & Children. Learn how to spell &
read the *Qur`ān* with us from the very beginning. Use *Fahm al-Qawā`id* 2019 © LEVEL ONE.

1 You deserve the best Islamic Education! Whether you are in school or
college or university you can start learning how to read *Qur`ān* here!

Fahm al-Qawā`id © 2019 أ ببتنجوغدنُرِرِتَش

Foundation Entry Level
First Edition
August 2018 - 2019

Published: PI
Copyright © 2019

2 فهمُ القَوَاعِدِ

Fahm al-Qawā`id

Name of Student:_____

Name of Teacher:_____

Year/Class:_____

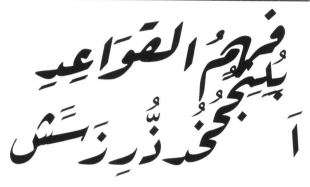

Foundation Entry Level - Arabic Alphabets & Words

A new *Qaidah* for a new way of learning *alhamdulillah* Fahm al-Qawā`id 2019 ©
Learning the letters of Arabic, vowel signs & translations of words.
Perfect choice for learning & teaching from the very beginning.

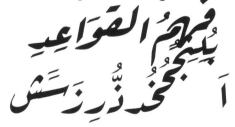

Learn & Understand
Qaida with Meanings

بِسْمِ اللهِ الرَّحْمنِ الرَّحِيْمِ

إنَّما الأعمال بالنيات

Table of Contents

فَهمُ القَوَاعِدِ

بسم الله الرحمن الرحيم

Introduction of Author

بسم الله الرحمن الرحيم

الحمد لله الحكيم الرزاق الذي أرسل الرسل بالهدى ودين الحق وأشهد. ألا إله إلا الله وحده لا شريك له وأشهد أن محمدا عبده ورسوله قدوة أهل الحكمة وأفضائل وله الأوصاف الجميلة والشمائل صلى الله عليه وعلى آله وأصحابه وسلم أما بعد:

The present day books from Bangladesh, Pakistan, India and the subcontinent have done a great service (there is no doubt) for passing on the knowledge of reading Qur`an to non-Arab communities in the West and non-Arab countries. I hope to add and share in the reward by adding to this service that our elders and teachers of the past and present have dedicated their lives for.

I have added translations to the new words. This is very unique as many students request to know the meaning of many words in the Qaida and, to my knowledge, the traditional Islamic evening and week-end Islamic schools do not provide this in their Qaida. I have tried to stick closely to using the Uthmani Script as much as possible. The book has been divided into eight sections. Each section consists of a number of lessons. Many unique features have been included. I have taken away some difficult *tajweed* rules which young kids, adults and new Arabic students will or may find difficult in comprehending.

I hope this will be of use and benefit for other students and teachers. I pray and hope that Allah will make this the best Qaidah series for the centuries and generations that follow. Perfection is with Allah and thus any mistakes found are from myself and anything good within then all praise is due to Allah

أسأل الله الكريم رب العرش العظيم لحسن الخاتمة، و جعله الله كتابا مباركا ونافعا للعالم والمسلمين، وأسأل الله تعالى أن يغفر لنا الزلل وأن يجعله من الأعمال التي لا تنقطع ويضع له القبول، وأسأل الله تعالى أن ينفع به مؤلفه وقارئه وأن يدخلنا الله الجنة بغير حساب ولا عناب إنه جواد كريم وصلى الله على نبينا محمد وعلى آله وصحبه الأخيار ومن تبعهم بإحسان.

Author

فهم القواعد ٥

The First Section

ابْتَثِجَّحَدِذِرِزِسَش

→ Lesson One: This lesson is for learning alphabets.

→ Lesson Two: This lesson is also for recognising the alphabets.

→ Lesson Three: This lesson includes a basic introduction to Alphabets with vowel signs such as *fatha, kasra* and *dhamma*.

→ Lesson Four: This lesson presents each letter three times in a row with vowel signs such as *fatha, kasra* and *dhamma*.

Starting Date of First Section:_____ **Final Grade for Section 1:**_____	
Teacher's comments	
Lesson One:	
Lesson Two:	
Lesson Three:	
Lesson Four:	

→ Tick stars given by teacher for Lesson One: *****   ****   ***   **   * ___

→ Tick stars given by teacher for Lesson Two: *****   ****   ***   **   * ___

→ Tick stars given by teacher for Lesson Three: *****   ****   ***   **   * ___

→ Tick stars given by teacher for Lesson Four: *****   ****   ***   **   * ___

Date completed:_____ Teacher's Signature:_____

بِسْمِ اللّٰهِ الرَّحْمٰنِ الرَّحِيمِ

THE FIRST SECTION - LESSON ONE (This lesson is for learning alphabets).

ا ب ت ث ج

ح خ د ذ ر

ز س ش ص ض

ط ظ ع غ ف

ق ك ل م ن

و ه ء ي

بِسْمِ اللّٰهِ الرَّحْمٰنِ الرَّحِيْمِ

THE FIRST SECTION - LESSON TWO (This lesson is for recognising the alphabets).

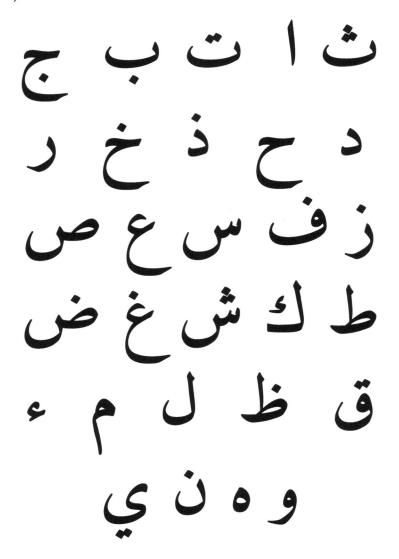

بِسْمِ اللّٰهِ الرَّحْمٰنِ الرَّحِيْمِ

THE FIRST SECTION - LESSON THREE (Introduction to vowel sign *fatha*)

أَ بَ تَ ثَ ثَ جَ

حَ خَ دَ ذَ رَ

زَ سَ شَ صَ ضَ

طَ ظَ عَ غَ فَ

قَ كَ لَ مَ نَ

وَ هَ ءَ يَ

٩ فَهْمُ القَوَاعِدِ

إِ بِ تِ تِ ثِ جِ

حِ خِ دِ ذِ رِ

زِ سِ شِ صِ ضِ

طِ ظِ عِ غِ فِ

قِ كِ لِ مِ نِ

وِ هِ ءِ يِ

جُ ثُ ثُ تُ بُ اُ

رُ ذُ دُ خُ حُ

ضُ صُ شُ سُ زُ

فُ غُ عُ ظُ طُ

نُ مُ لُ كُ قُ

يُ ءُ هُ وُ

فَهمُ القَوَاعِدِ 11

بِسْمِ اللّٰهِ الرَّحْمٰنِ الرَّحِيْمِ

THE FIRST SECTION - LESSON FOUR (Presenting each letter three times with vowel signs).

اَ اِ اُ بَ بِ بُ

تَ تِ تُ

ثَ ثِ ثُ جَ جِ جُ

حَ حِ حُ خَ خِ خُ

دَ دِ دُ ذَ ذِ ذُ رَ رِ رُ

سُ سِ سَ زُ زِ زَ

شُ شِ شَ

صُ صِ صَ

ضُ ضِ ضَ

ظُ ظِ ظَ طُ طِ طَ

غُ غِ غَ عُ عِ عَ

فَ فِ فُ قَ قِ قُ

كَ كِ كُ لَ لِ لُ

مَ مِ مُ نَ نِ نُ

وَ وِ وُ هَ هِ هُ ءَ ءِ ءُ

يَ يِ يُ

Please revise all previous lessons properly before moving to the next sections.

May Allah grant us and you all success in both worlds.

The Second Section

ابْتَثُخَدْ ذَر زِسَش

→This lesson shows us how the Arabic letters look like when they are joined from the front. Some do not join.

→ This lesson shows us how the Arabic letters look like when they are joined from behind.

→ This lesson shows us how the Arabic letters look like when they are joined from both sides. Some do not join from both sides.

Starting Date of Section Section:_____**Final Grade for Section 2:**_____

Teacher's comments

Lesson One:

Lesson Two:

Lesson Three:

→ Tick stars given by teacher for Lesson One: *****   ****   ***   **   *__

→ Tick stars given by teacher for Lesson Two: *****   ****   ***   **   *__

→ Tick stars given by teacher for Lesson Three: *****   ****   ***   **   *__

Date completed:_____Teacher's Signature:_____

بِسْمِ اللّٰهِ الرَّحْمٰنِ الرَّحِيْمِ

THE SECOND SECTION - LESSON ONE (How Arabic letters look when they are joined from the front. Some do not join).

ا بـ تـ ثـ جـ

حـ خـ د ذ ر

ز سـ شـ صـ ضـ

طـ ظـ عـ غـ ف

قـ كـ لـ مـ نـ

و هـ ئـ يـ

بِسْمِ اللّٰهِ الرَّحْمٰنِ الرَّحِيْم

THE SECOND SECTION - LESSON TWO (The Arabic letters when they are joined from behind).

ج ﺚ ﺖ ﺐ ﺎ

ﺮ ﺬ ﺪ ﺦ ﺢ

ﺾ ﺺ ﺶ ﺲ ﺰ

ﻒ ﻎ ﻊ ﻆ ﻂ

ﻦ ﻢ ﻞ ﻚ ﻖ

ﻲ ﺊ ﻪ ﻮ

بِسْمِ اللّٰهِ الرَّحْمٰنِ الرَّحِيْمِ

THE SECOND SECTION - LESSON THREE (How Arabic letters look joined from both sides).

جـ ثـ تـ بـ ـا

ر ذ د خـ حـ

ضـ صـ شـ سـ ز

فـ غـ عـ ظـ طـ

نـ مـ لـ كـ قـ

يـ ئـ هـ و

The Third Section

ابـحـخـذ ذ ر ز ـس ش

→ This lesson consists of some letters in a different form that students may find confusing. Please explain and teach each letter. Highlight the differences between these letters and other forms.

→ This part includes new words along with their translation. This section will only introduce words that have a fatha on each of its letters.

→ The next part includes new words along with their translation. This section will only introduce words that have fathas on its letters and kasras.

→ The next part includes new words along with their translation. This section will only introduce words that have fathas, kasras and dhammas.

Starting Date of Third Section:_____**Final Grade for Section 3:**_____

Teacher's comments

Lesson One:

Lesson Two:

Lesson Three:

Lesson Four:

→ Tick stars given by teacher for Lesson One: ***** **** *** ** * __

→ Tick stars given by teacher for Lesson Two: ***** **** *** ** * __

→ Tick stars given by teacher for Lesson Three: ***** **** *** ** * __

→ Tick stars given by teacher for Lesson Four: ***** **** *** ** * __

Date completed:_____Teacher's Signature:_____

بِسْمِ اللّٰهِ الرَّحْمٰنِ الرَّحِيْمِ

THE THIRD SECTION - LESSON ONE (This lessons consists of some letters in a different form that students may find confusing. Please explain and teach each letter. Highlight the differences between these letters and other forms).

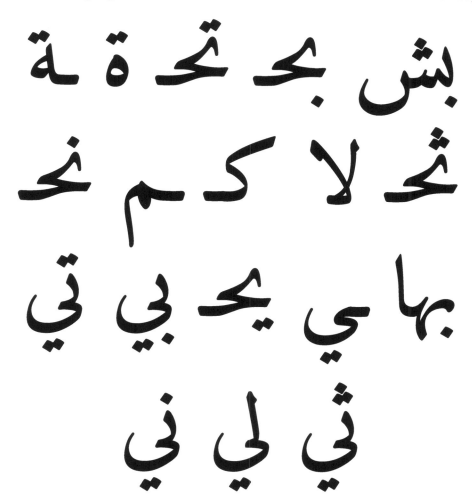

بش بح تح ة ة ة

ثح لا ك م نح

بها ي يح بي تي

ثي لي ني

بِسْمِ اللّٰهِ الرَّحْمٰنِ الرَّحِيْمِ

THE THIRD SECTION - LESSON TWO (This part includes new words along with their translation. This section will only introduce words that have fathas on each of its letters).

جَعَلَ	تَرَكَ	بَلَغَ	أَمَرَ
He has made (or) He has gathered	He left	He reached	He ordered
ذَهَبَ	دَرَسَ	خَلَقَ	حَضَرَ
He went	He studied	He created	He attended
رَجَعَ	زَعَمَ	سَجَدَ	وَجَدَ
He returned	He claimed	He prostrated	He found

طَلَبَ	شَرَعَ	صَبَرَ	ضَرَبَ
He sought (or) He requested	He legislated (or) He started	He was patient	He hit (or) He struck

ظَهَرَ	أَكَلَ	غَسَلَ	فَتَحَ
He appeared	He ate	He washed	He opened

قَرَأَ	كَتَبَ	لَعَنَ	مَنَعَ	نَظَرَ
He read	He wrote	He cursed	He prevented	He looked

بِسْمِ اللّٰهِ الرَّحْمٰنِ الرَّحِيمِ

THE THIRD SECTION - LESSON THIRD (The next part includes new words along with their translation. This section will only introduce words that have fathas on its letters and kasras).

أَذِنَ	عَلِمَ	لَعِبَ	حَمِدَ
He permitted	He knew	He played	He praised

فَهِمَ	تَعِبَ	عَمِلَ	شَرِبَ
He understood	He became tired	He worked	He drank

لَقِيَ	سَمِعَ	لَقِيَ	غَضِبَ
He met	He heard	He met	He became angry

خَشِيَ	عَجِبَ	كَذِبَ	بَخِلَ
He feared	He became amazed	He lied	He withheld

بِسْمِ اللّٰهِ الرَّحْمٰنِ الرَّحِيْمِ

THE THIRD SECTION - LESSON FOUR (The next part includes new words along with their translation. This section will only introduce words that have fathas, kasras and dhammas).

كُتِبَ	ظُلِمَ	مُنِعَ	خُلِقَ
It was written	He was oppressed	He was prevented	It was created

رُزِقَ	فُتِحَ	قُطِعَ	فُرِضَ
He was provided	It was opened	It was cut	It was made obligatory

ضُرِبَ	رُسُلُهُ	كُتُبُهُ	شُرِبَ
He was hit	His Messengers	His Books	It was drunk

The Fourth Section

ابتَّخُذَرزِش

→ Extra practice.

→ An introduction to double *fatha* known also as *fathatayn*.

→An introduction to double *kasra* known also as *kasratayn*.

→An introduction to double *dhamma* known also as *dhammatayn*.

Starting Date of The Fourth Section:_____Final Grade for Section 4:_____

Teacher's comments

Lesson One:

Lesson Two:

Lesson Three:

Lesson Four:

→ Tick stars given by teacher for Lesson One: *****   ****   ***   **   * __

→ Tick stars given by teacher for Lesson Two: *****   ****   ***   **   * __

→ Tick stars given by teacher for Lesson Three: *****   ****   ***   **   * __

→ Tick stars given by teacher for Lesson Four: *****   ****   ***   **   * __

Date completed:_____Teacher's Signature:_____

بِسْمِ اللّٰهِ الرَّحْمٰنِ الرَّحِيمِ

THE FOURTH SECTION - LESSON ONE (Extra practice).

مَعَهُ	لَكَ	بِهَا	لَهُ	هِيَ
With him	For you	With it/her	Belongs to Him	She is/It is
لَعَنَ	فَسَدَ	حَسَدَ	شَرِبَ	عَمِلَ
He cursed	He corrupted	He envied	He drank	He worked
صَدَقَ	قَطَعَ	شَرَعَ	فَتَحَ	ذَهَبَ
He spoke the truth	He cut	He started	He opened	He went
شَرَحَ	نَسِيَ	رُسُلٌ	يَدُهُ	وَجَدَ
He explained	He forgot	Messengers	His hand	He found

بِسْمِ اللّٰهِ الرَّحْمٰنِ الرَّحِيْمِ

THE FOURTH SECTION - LESSON TWO (Introduction to double fatha known as fathatayn).

أَ بَا تَا ثَا جَا حَا خَا دَا

ذَا رَا زَا سَا شَا صَا ضَا

طَا ظَا عَا غَا فَا قَا كَا

لَا مَا نَا وَا هَا ئَا يَا

بِسْمِ اللّٰهِ الرَّحْمٰنِ الرَّحِيْمِ

THE FOURTH SECTION - LESSON THREE (Introduction to kasratayn).

خِ حِ جِ ثِ تِ بِ إِ

صِ شِ سِ زِ رِ ذِ دِ

فِ غِ عِ ظِ طِ ضِ

مِ لِ كِ قِ

يِ ءِ هِ وِ نِ

بِسْمِ اللّهِ الرَّحْمنِ الرَّحِيْمِ

THE FOURTH SECTION - LESSON FOUR (Introduction to double dhamma known as dhammatayn).

The Fifth Section

ابتجمخدذرزسش

→ This lesson presents each word with *fathas*, *dhammas*, *kasras* and *fathatayn* with translation.

→ This lesson presents each word with *fathas*, *dhammas*, *kasras* and *kasratayn* with translation.

→ This lesson presents each word with *fathas*, *dhammas*, *kasras* and *dhammatayn* with translation.

→ This lesson presents 3 words next to each other with different endings. No translation will be provided.

Starting Date of The Fifth Section:_____**Final Grade for Section 5:**_____   **Teacher's comments**   Lesson One: Lesson Two: Lesson Three: Lesson Four:

→ Tick stars given by teacher for Lesson One: *****   ****   ***   **   * __
→ Tick stars given by teacher for Lesson Two: *****   ****   ***   **   * __
→ Tick stars given by teacher for Lesson Three: *****   ****   ***   **   * __
→ Tick stars given by teacher for Lesson Four: *****   ****   ***   **   * __

Date completed:_____Teacher's Signature:_____

بِسْمِ اللّٰهِ الرَّحْمٰنِ الرَّحِيْمِ

THE FIFTH SECTION - LESSON ONE (This lesson presents each word with *fathas*, *dhammas*, *kasras* and *fathatayn* with translation).

سُبُلًا	أَلِيمًا	رُسُلًا	بَقَرَةً
Paths	**Painful**	**Messengers**	**A Cow**
حَسَنَةً	عَلَقَةً	عِنَبًا	ثَمَنًا
Good	**(Into) a clinging substance**	**Grape**	**(for) a price**
لَعِبًا	أَحَدًا	حَزَنًا	شَجَرَةً
(as) a play	**anyone**	**Sorrow**	**A tree**
سُفُنًا	دَرَجَةً	كَذِبًا	طَبَقًا
Ships	**A mark or a level**	**A lie**	**(from) stage (to stage)**

بِسْمِ اللّٰهِ الرَّحْمٰنِ الرَّحِيْمِ

THE FIFTH SECTION - LESSON TWO (This lesson presents each word with *fathas, dhammas, kasras* and *kasratayn* with translation).

سَنَةٍ	حَسَنٍ	رُسُلٍ	خَبَرٍ
A year	Good	Messengers	Information
فَتَحٍ	عَلَقَةٍ	بَبِبٍ	سُسَسٍ
---	A blood clot	---	---
بَلَدٍ	عِنَبٍ	شَجَرَةٍ	حَرَمٍ
A country	Grapes	A tree	Sanctuary
وَرَقٍ	جَرَسٍ	عَعُعٍ	كُتُبٍ
Paper	A bell	---	Books

فَهْمُ الْقَوَاعِدِ 33

بِسْمِ اللّٰهِ الرَّحْمٰنِ الرَّحِيْمِ

THE FIFTH SECTION - LESSON THREE (This lesson presents each word with *fathas*, *dhammas*, *kasras* and *dhammatayn* with translation).

قَلَمٌ A pen	حَطَبٌ Firewood	لَبَنٌ Milk	طَلَبٌ A request
كُتُبٌ A book	يَدٌ A hand	حَلَبٌ Aleppo (name of city)	حَمَدٌ Hamad (A name)
قَلَمٌ A pen	جَبَلٌ A mountain	مُدُنٌ Cities	رُسُلٌ Messengers
لَبَنٌ Milk	فِيْلٌ An elephant	مُسْلِمٌ A Muslim	حَجَرٌ A stone

بِسْمِ اللّٰهِ الرَّحْمٰنِ الرَّحِيمِ

THE FIFTH SECTION - LESSON FOUR (This lesson presents 3 words next to each other with the same meaning but different ending).

سُبُلًا سُبُلٍ سُبُلٌ بَقَرَةً بَقَرَةٍ بَقَرَةٌ

A cow ------------------------- Paths

رُسُلًا رُسُلٍ رُسُلٌ أَلِيمًا أَلِيمٍ أَلِيمٌ

Painful ------------------------- Messengers

مُسْلِمًا مُسْلِمٍ مُسْلِمٌ طَلَبًا طَلَبٍ طَلَبٌ

A request ------------------------- A Muslim

مُدُنًا مُدُنٍ مُدُنٌ قَلَمًا قَلَمٍ قَلَمٌ

A pen------------------------- Cities

كُتُبًا كُتُبٍ كُتُبٌ لَبَنًا لَبَنٍ لَبَنٌ

Milk ------------------------- Books

حَجَرًا حَجَرٍ حَجَرٌ بَصَلًا بَصَلٍ بَصَلٌ

Onions ------------------------- A stone

The Sixth Section

ابحخذدرزسش

→ This lesson we introduce the letter of *alif mad*.

→ This lesson we introduce the letter of *alif mad* inside words.

Starting Date of The Sixth Section:_____**Final Grade for Section 6:**_____

Teacher's comments

Lesson One:

Lesson Two:

→ Tick stars given by teacher for Lesson One: ***** **** *** ** * __

→ Tick stars given by teacher for Lesson Two: ***** **** *** ** * __

Date completed:_____Teacher's Signature:_____

بِسْمِ اللّٰهِ الرَّحْمٰنِ الرَّحِيْمِ

THE SIXTH SECTION - LESSON ONE (This lesson we introduce the letter *alif mad*).

$$\text{تا} = \text{ا} + \text{ت} \quad * \quad \text{با} = \text{ا} + \text{ب}$$

$$\text{ثا} = \text{ا} + \text{ث}$$

جا حا خا دا ذا را زا

سا شا صا ضا طا ظا

عا غا فا قا كا لا ما وا

ها ئا يا

Fahm al-Qawā`id © 2019

بِسْمِ اللّٰهِ الرَّحْمٰنِ الرَّحِيْمِ

THE SIXTH SECTION - LESSON TWO (This lesson we introduce the letter alif *mad* inside words).

حَارٌّ   جَاءَ   زَادَ   تَاجِرٌ   بَابٌ

Hot   He came   He Increased   Business Man   A door

شَاءَ   رَانَ   جَارٌ   دَارٌ   خَابَ

He wills   Covered   Neighbour   A home   He failed

غَافِرٌ   عَادِلٌ   ظَالِمٌ   طَائِرٌ   صَارَ

Forgiving   Just   An oppressor   A bird   He became

Please revise all previous lessons properly before moving to the next sections.

The Seventh Section

اَلْبَخَذَرزَسْ

→This lesson introduces the *sukoon* and the *hamza alif* with *fatha*.
→This lesson introduces the *sukoon* and the *hamza alif* with *dhamma*.
→This lesson introduces the *sukoon* and the *hamza alif* with *kasra*.
→This lesson introduces many words with sukoon in different ways.

Starting Date of The Seventh Section:_____Final Grade for Section 7:_____

Teacher's comments

Lesson One:

Lesson Two:

Lesson Three:

Lesson Four:

→ Tick stars given by teacher for Lesson One: *****   ****   ***   **   * __
→ Tick stars given by teacher for Lesson Two: *****   ****   ***   **   * __
→ Tick stars given by teacher for Lesson Three: *****   ****   ***   **   * __
→ Tick stars given by teacher for Lesson Four: *****   ****   ***   **   * __

Date completed:_____Teacher's Signature:_____

بِسْمِ اللّٰهِ الرَّحْمٰنِ الرَّحِيْمِ

THE SEVENTH SECTION - LESSON ONE (This lesson introduces the *sukoon* and the *hamza alif* with *fatha*).

أَجْ أَثْ أَتْ أَبْ

أَرْ أَذْ أَدْ أَخْ أَحْ

أَضْ أَصْ أَشْ أَسْ أَزْ

أَقْ أَفْ أَغْ أَعْ أَظْ أَطْ

أَيْ أَهْ أَوْ أَنْ أَمْ أَلْ أَكْ

بِسْمِ اللّٰهِ الرَّحْمٰنِ الرَّحِيْمِ

THE SEVENTH SECTION - LESSON TWO (This lesson introduces the *sukoon* and the *hamza alif* with *dhamma*.).

أُبْ أُتْ أَتْ أُثْ أَجْ أَحْ

أُخْ أُدْ أَذْ أُرْ أَزْ أَسْ أَثْ

أُصْ أَضْ أَطْ أُظْ أَعْ

أُغْ أُفْ أَقْ أَكْ أُلْ أَمْ

أَنْ أُوْ أَهْ أُيْ

بِسْمِ اللّٰهِ الرَّحْمٰنِ الرَّحِيْمِ

THE SEVENTH SECTION - LESSON THREE (This lesson introduces the *sukoon* and the *hamza alif* with *kasra*).

إِبْ إِتْ إِتْ إِثْ إِجْ إِحْ

إِخْ إِذْ إِذْ إِرْ إِزْ إِسْ إِشْ

إِصْ إِضْ إِطْ إِظْ إِعْ

إِغْ إِفْ إِقْ إِكْ إِلْ إِمْ

إِنْ إِوْ إِهْ إِيْ

بِسْمِ اللّٰهِ الرَّحْمٰنِ الرَّحِيْمِ

THE SEVENTH SECTION - LESSON FOUR (This lesson introduces many words with sukoon in different ways).

تَوْبَةٌ	بَيْتٌ	رَيْبٌ	أَبِيْ
Repentance	A house	Doubt	My father

زِدْنِيْ	تُبْ وَخُذْ	أَوْ	أَمْ
Increase me	Repent & take	Or	Or

قَلْبِيْ	يَشْرَبُ	كُلْ لَهُمْ	كَمْ وَقُلْ
My heart	He is drinking	Eat for them	How much & say

يَأْتِيْ	يُؤْمِنُ	قَرَأْتُ	أُوْحِيَ
He is coming	He believes	I read	It was revealed

خَيْرًا	قُرَيْشٌ	أَهْلِي	كَأْسٌ
Good	Quraysh	My family	A cup
قَوْلٌ	اَلْإِسْلَامُ	أُوْتِيَ قَلَمٌ	أَوْ فِي
A statement	Al-Islaam	He was given a pen	Or in
دِيْنِي	عَيْنِي	نُوْرٌ	قِيْلَ
My religion	My eye	Light	It was said

Fahm al-Qawā`id © 2019 اَبْتَحْخَدْ ذَرِ زَسْش

The Eighth Section

اَبْتَحْخَد ذَرِ زَسْش

→This lesson introduces standing *fatha* inside basic words and *hamzatul wasl*.

→This lesson introduces standing *kasra* and reverse *dhamma* and a few words with them.

→This lesson introduces *shadda* with *fatha, kasra, dhamma* on it and before it.

→This lesson introduces *shadda* with *fatha, kasra, dhamma* on it and before it.

→ This lesson introduces *shadda* in words, with *madd,* various vowels and standing *fatha* on *shadda*.

→ Various small sentences preparing the student for level 2 and in class education of further tajweed rules. After this lesson the student can use our level 2 or use any *juzz amma* book. After level 2 the student should be ready to slowly move on to reading the Qur`an In-Shaa-Allah.

Starting Date of The Eighth Section:_____Final Grade for Section 8:_____

Teacher's comments

Lesson One:

Lesson Two:

Lesson Three:

Lesson Four:

The Final Lesson:

→ Tick stars given by teacher for Lesson One: ***** **** *** ** * __

→ Tick stars given by teacher for Lesson Two: ***** **** *** ** * __

→ Tick stars given by teacher for Lesson Three: ***** **** *** ** * __

→ Tick stars given by teacher for Lesson Four: ***** **** *** ** * __

→ Tick stars given by teacher for Final Lesson: ***** **** *** ** * __

Date completed:_____Teacher's Signature:_____

بِسْمِ اللّٰهِ الرَّحْمٰنِ الرَّحِيْمِ

THE EIGHTH SECTION - LESSON ONE (This lesson introduces standing *fatha* inside basic words and hamzatul wasl). Please explain this lesson carefully to your students so that there is no misunderstanding.

اٰ بٰ تٰ ثٰ جٰ حٰ خٰ دٰ

ذٰ رٰ زٰ سٰ شٰ صٰ ضٰ

طٰ ظٰ عٰ غٰ فٰ قٰ كٰ

لٰ مٰ نٰ وٰ يٰ

ذٰلِكَ ٱلۡكِتٰبُ

That is the Book

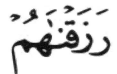

We have provided them

God (or Deity)

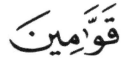

Stand out firmly

وَالْمَسْجِدُ	وَالْقَمَرُ	وَالْبَيْتُ	وَالْكِتَابُ
And the Mosque	And the moon	And the house	And the book

وَالْجَمَلُ	وَالْمَوْزُ	وَالْأَبُ	وَالْمِفْتَاحُ
And the camel	And the banana	And the father	And the key

بِسْمِ اللّٰهِ الرَّحْمٰنِ الرَّحِيْمِ

THE EIGHTH SECTION - LESSON TWO (This lesson introduces standing *kasra* and reverse *dhamma* and a few words with them).

خُ حُ جُ ثُ ثِ تِ بِ اِ

ي ه ت ت ث ت ب ا

يْ هْ ضْ صْ شْ سْ زْ رْ

بَيْتُهُ يَدُهُ الْفِ هٰذِهِ ذٰلِكَ

يَرَهُ دَاوُدُ

بِسْمِ اللّٰهِ الرَّحْمٰنِ الرَّحِيْم

THE EIGHTH SECTION - LESSON THREE (This lesson introduces *shadda* with *fatha*, *kasra*, *dhamma* on it and before it). Please note the kasra can go below the letter or below the shadda please explain this to your student.

أَبَّ أَبِّ أَبُّ إِتَّ إِتِّ إِتُّ

أَجَّ أَجِّ أَجُّ أَخَّ أَخِّ أَخُّ أَدَّ أَدِّ أَدُّ

أَزَّ أَزِّ أَزُّ أَسَّ أَشِّ أَشُّ أَصَّ

أَضِّ أَضُّ أَطَّ أَظَّ أَغُّ أَفَّ أَفِّ

أَفُّ أَلَّ إِلَّ أُلُّ مَنَّ أَمَّ بَيَّ بَيِّ

أَيُّ

بِسْمِ اللّٰهِ الرَّحْمٰنِ الرَّحِيمِ

THE EIGHTH SECTION - LESSON FOUR (This lesson introduces *shadda* in words, with *madd,* various vowels and standing *fatha* on *shadda*).

عَمٌّ	اَللّٰهُ	ثُمَّ	حَقٌّ
Paternal Uncle	Allah	Then	Truth
حُبُّ اللّٰهِ	مُحَمَّدٌ	شَرٌّ	دَمَّرَ
Love of Allah	Muhammad	Evil	He destroyed
اَلنَّبِيُّ	نَبِيُّ اللّٰهِ	إِلَّا	مِنَّا
The Prophet	The Prophet of Allah	Except	From us
عَلَّمَ	اَلدِّينُ	اَلرَّبُّ	عَنِّي
He taught	The Religion	The Lord	About me

بِسْمِ اللّٰهِ الرَّحْمٰنِ الرَّحِيمِ

THE EIGHTH SECTION - FINAL LESSON (various small sentences preparing the student for level 2 and in class education of further tajweed rules. After this lesson the student can use our level 2 or use any *juzz amma*. After level 2 the student should be ready to slowly move on to reading the *Qur`an*). This is a test so there will be no meanings provided. The aim of this lesson is to check your reading which is the main purpose. This lesson is difficult because of the actual Uthmani Qur'anic Script provided.

جُنَاحَ

وَٱلْكِتَٰبِ ٱلْمُبِينِ

مَا لَمْ تَمَسُّوهُنَّ

قُلْ أَعُوذُ بِرَبِّ ٱلنَّاسِ

وَمِن شَرِّ غَاسِقٍ إِذَا وَقَبَ

خَلَقَ ٱلسَّمَوَاتِ وَٱلْأَرْضَ

بِٱلْحَقِّ تَعَلَىٰ عَمَّا يُشْرِكُونَ

وَٱتَّقُوا۟ ٱللَّهَ إِنَّ ٱللَّهَ شَدِيدُ ٱلْعِقَابِ

Final Report for Student Progress and Teachers's Comments:

_____

_____

_____

_____

_____

_____

_____

_____

_____

_____

*Teacher's Signature:*_____*Date:*_____

Fahm al-Qawā`id

Start learning how to spell & read the Qur`ān!
Starting from Alif Bā Tā, then words & their meanings!

Foundation Entry Level - Understanding Qaida

A new Qaidah for a new way of learning *alhamdulillah* Fahm al-Qawā`id 2019 ©
Learning the letters of Arabic, vowel signs & translations of words.
Perfect choice for learning & teaching from the very beginning.

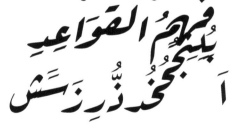

Learn & Understand
Qaida with Meanings

Other books available by the same author:

More books for Children:

- Fahm al-Qawā`id © 2019 (Black & White Version).
- Fahm al-Qawā`id © 2019 (Colour Version).
- To be published soon InShāAllah.

Academic writings:

- The Prophets and Their Divine Message.
- 6 Academic Essays on Islamic Studies for University Students and Higher Education in the West.

More coming soon InShāAllah

46557589R00034

Printed in Poland
by Amazon Fulfillment
Poland Sp. z o.o., Wrocław